UNDERSTANDING ANXIETY

WHAT IS ANXIETY?

CAITIE MCANENEY

PowerKiDS press.

NEW YORK

Published in 2021 by The Rosen Publishing Group, Inc.
29 East 21st Street, New York, NY 10010

Copyright © 2021 by The Rosen Publishing Group, Inc.

All rights reserved. No part of this book may be reproduced in any form without permission in writing from the publisher, except by a reviewer.

First Edition

Editor: Kristen Susienka
Book Design: Rachel Rising

Photo Credits: Cover, p.15, Africa Studio/Shutterstock.com; Cover, fizkes/Shutterstock.com; Cover, mtkang/Shutterstock.com; Cover Matt Benoit/Shutterstock.com; Cover, pp. 1,3,4,6,8,10,12,14,16,18,20,22,23,24 (background) Flas100/Shutterstock.com Cover, pp. 1,3,5,6,9,11,13,15,17,19,21(textbook) mhatzapa/Shutterstock.com; p.4 Jelena Aloskina/Shutterstock.com; pp. 5,21 Monkey Business Images/Shutterstock.com; p. 7 Tero Vesalainen/Shutterstock.com; p. 8 dizain/Shutterstock.com; pp. 9,18 New Africa/Shutterstock.com; p. 10 Audrey SniderBell/Shutterstock.com; p. 11 Zivica Kerkez/Shutterstock.com; p. 12 kwanchai.c/Shutterstock.com; p. 13 PixelShot/Shutterstock.com; p. 16 Aila Images/Shutterstock.com; p. 17 Iakov Filimonov/Shutterstock.com; p. 19 kryzhov/Shutterstock.com; p. 20 VaLiza/Shutterstock.com; p. 22 michaeljung/Shutterstock.com.

Some of the images in this book illustrate individuals who are models. The depictions do not imply actual situations or events.

Library of Congress Cataloging-in-Publication Data

Names: McAneney, Caitie, author.
Title: What is anxiety? / Caitie McAneney.
Description: New York : PowerKids Press, [2021] | Series: Understanding
    anxiety | Includes index.
Identifiers: LCCN 2019051177 | ISBN 9781725318052 (paperback) | ISBN
    9781725318076 (library binding) | ISBN 9781725318069 (6 pack)
Subjects: LCSH: Anxiety in children—Juvenile literature.
Classification: LCC BF723.A5 M38 2021 | DDC 155.4/1246–dc23
LC record available at https://lccn.loc.gov/2019051177

Manufactured in the United States of America

CPSIA Compliance Information: Batch #CSPK20. For Further Information contact Rosen Publishing, New York, New York at 1-800-237-9932.

Find us on

CONTENTS

WHAT IS ANXIETY?................................4

WHAT DOES ANXIETY FEEL LIKE?.....................6

WHAT IFS..8

ANXIETY AND THE BRAIN..........................10

DIFFERENT KINDS OF ANXIETY.....................12

GIVING YOUR ANXIETY A NAME.....................14

FEELING BETTER.................................16

CALMING DOWN...................................18

HELPING OTHERS WITH ANXIETY....................20

OVERCOMING ANXIETY.............................22

GLOSSARY.......................................23

WEBSITES.......................................24

INDEX..24

WHAT IS ANXIETY?

Imagine you have to present a paper in class. As you walk to the front of the room, your hands start to sweat and your heart pounds. You feel shaky and dizzy. You might be feeling anxiety.

Anxiety is worrying, feeling afraid, or feeling nervous. Everyone is anxious sometimes. However, sometimes anxiety makes it hard to go to school, make new friends, or try new things. If this is how you or a friend is feeling, you or they may have anxiety.

WHAT DOES ANXIETY FEEL LIKE?

What does it feel like to have anxiety? Some symptoms, or signs, are things that you feel in your body. Some symptoms of anxiety are feeling dizzy or having **tingling** fingers and toes, having a stomachache, or a tight feeling in your chest.

Anxiety can make your heart beat harder and faster than normal. You might find it hard to sleep or eat. You might feel warm or start to sweat. It might be hard to breathe normally or **concentrate** on what you're supposed to be doing.

A SUDDEN, INTENSE FEELING OF ANXIETY, OFTEN WITH NO REASON, IS CALLED A PANIC ATTACK. **PHYSICAL** SYMPTOMS COME ON FAST AND CAN BE VERY SCARY, BUT THEY DON'T LAST VERY LONG.

WHAT IFS

Someone with an anxiety problem might feel very scared that something bad is going to happen. They might have racing thoughts, full of "what-ifs." What if no one likes me? What if people make fun of me for not scoring that goal? What if I get into a car accident? These thoughts set off a physical reaction.

Sometimes, people with anxiety can't stop thinking about something and try to do certain actions to stop the thoughts. This may be obsessive-compulsive disorder.

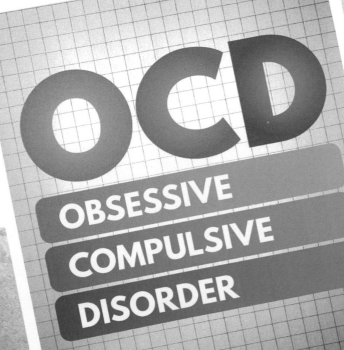

ANXIETY AND THE BRAIN

The physical and **mental** feelings that come with anxiety have to do with how the brain works. When something scares us, we often have a fight-or-flight **response**. That means our body gets ready to either fight the **threat** or run away.

This reaction causes a rush of something called **adrenaline**. It makes your heart pound and your mind direct attention on the threat. This was helpful for our **ancestors**, who had to fight wild animals. However, today a fight-or-flight response can just make us feel more anxious!

 Rattlesnake →

DIFFERENT KINDS OF ANXIETY

Anxiety disorders come in different forms. Generalized anxiety disorder means a person worries a lot of the time, about many things. They think about the worst things that could happen, even if they're not likely.

Some people have phobias, or fears of certain things. Someone might have a phobia of dogs or a fear of heights. Other people are afraid of being around other people in certain settings, which is called social anxiety. Some people have panic disorder, or panic attacks that happen often.

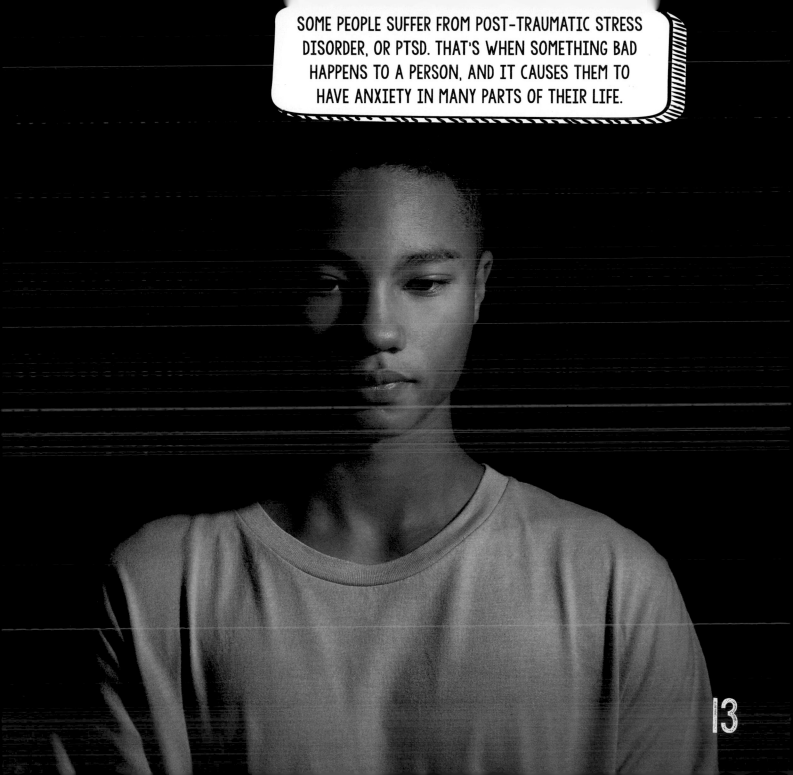

GIVING YOUR ANXIETY A NAME

You might go to your usual doctor or a kind of doctor called a psychologist to talk about your anxiety. Doctors usually treat issues inside your body. Psychologists or **counselors** can help treat issues within your mind. Both can help you through your anxiety.

First, they will gather information, or facts, about how you're feeling. They might ask you questions and gather information from your parents. Then, they'll make a diagnosis, or tell you what might be wrong. Sometimes it helps just to give a name to what you're feeling.

FEELING BETTER

Luckily, there are many ways to treat anxiety. Your doctor, psychologist, or counselor might suggest talk therapy. That's where you meet with a professional to talk about what you're feeling. You might learn how to replace unhelpful patterns of thinking and acting with healthy ones. You might learn different tools for dealing with anxiety and calming down.

Sometimes, a professional might give you **medicine** for anxiety. It can be used with talk therapy. There's no shame in taking medicine for anxiety!

CALMING DOWN

What are some tools you can use to calm down? You can write or draw your thoughts or feelings. You can also use your breath!

Focus on deep breathing. Take a "belly breath." Put your hand on your belly and let it get bigger as you breathe in and get smaller as you breathe out. Breathe in slowly, then let all the air out slowly. Count as you breathe. Try breathing in for four counts and out for six or eight counts.

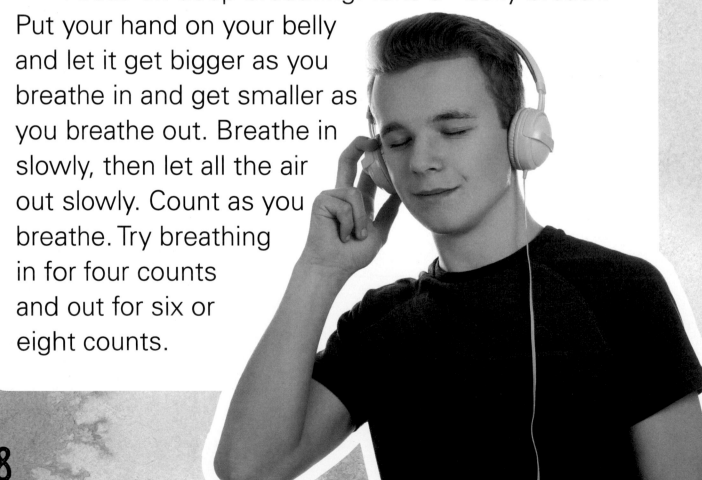

HELPING OTHERS WITH ANXIETY

Maybe you don't have anxiety, but you have a friend who does. How can you help them?

The best thing you can do is listen to your friend without judgment. People who feel anxiety sometimes feel embarrassed to talk about it. Having a friend who won't shame them about anxiety can be very helpful.

Talk to your friend about getting help from a parent or teacher. Let them know that there are mental health professionals who can help!

OVERCOMING ANXIETY

Even famous people, such as Lady Gaga and Ariana Grande, have struggled with anxiety. You can still reach your goals and live a full life even if you feel anxious. Remember, anxiety is something you feel, not who you are.

Once you learn tools for keeping calm, you can better deal with all kinds of things—in school, at home, and everywhere in between. The best way to overcome anxiety is to talk about it. The more people talk about it, the more normal it becomes!

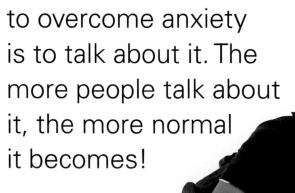

GLOSSARY

adrenaline: A matter that's part of the body's response to strong emotion.

ancestor: Someone who has come before you in a family line.

concentrate: To focus, or direct, one's attention.

counselor: A person who provides advice as part of their job.

embarrassed: Feeling or showing awareness for something you believe you've done wrong.

emotion: A state of feeling.

medicine: Pills or a drink given to someone who is sick to help them feel better.

mental: Of or relating to the mind.

physical: Relating to the body instead of the mind.

professional: Someone who does something for a living.

response: Saying or doing something in return, especially to a question or statement.

threat: Something that might hurt you.

tingling: Describing a slight feeling in one's body, such as stinging, prickling, or ringing.

INDEX

A

adrenaline, 10

B

brain, 10

C

counselor, 14, 16

D

diagnosis, 14
doctor, 14, 16

F

fight-or-flight response, 10, 11

G

generalized anxiety disorder, 12

H

heart, 6, 10

M

medicine, 16

O

obsessive-compulsive disorder, 8

P

panic attack, 6, 12

panic disorder, 12

phobias, 12

post-traumatic stress disorder (PTSD), 13

psychologist, 14, 16

R

racing thoughts, 8

S

social anxiety, 12

stomachache, 6

symptoms, 6

T

talk therapy, 16

WEBSITES

Due to the changing nature of Internet links, PowerKids Press has developed an online list of websites related to the subject of this book. This site is updated regularly. Please use this link to access the list: www.powerkidslinks.com/ua/anxiety